HIGH PROTEIN LOW CARB DIET COOKBOOK:

RECIPES TO HELP TONE YOU UP AND GIVE YOU YOUR SLIM AND SEXY BODY THROUGH EVERY SEASON.

By
JESSICA CAYWOOD

HIGH PROTEIN LOW CARB

Copyright © 2019, By: **JESSICA CAYWOOD**

ISBN-13: 978-1-950772-08-7
ISBN-10: 1-950772-08-X

All Rights Reserved. No part of this publication may be reproduced in any form or by any means, including scanning, photocopying, or otherwise without prior written permission of the copyright holder.

Disclaimer:
The information provided in this book is designed to provide helpful information on the subjects discussed. The publisher and author are not responsible for any specific health or allergy needs that may require medical supervision and are not liable for any damages or negative consequences from any treatment, action, application or preparation, to any person reading or following the information in this book.

HIGH PROTEIN LOW CARB

Table of Contents

THE HIGH PROTEIN LOW CARB DIET RECIPES TO HELP TONE YOU UP AND GIVE YOU YOUR SLIM AND SEXY BODY THROUGH EVERY SEASON 5
Badass Curried Chicken Fried "Rice" with Thai Coconut-Almond Sauce 7
Cave girl Eats' Badass Chili 9
Kenzie's Steak Salad 10
Breakfast for Dinner 11
No-Delivery Pizza 12
Chicken-Black Bean-Rice Bowl 13
Hamm Cheese-Stuffed Chicken 14
Gluten Free Sweet Potato Muffins 15
Badass Blueberry Protein Pancakes 17
Roasted Sweet Potato Soup 18
Twisted Tuna Salad 20
Chicken Caesar (The power salad) 21
Greek Salad 22
Flank Steak Chopped Steakhouse Salad 23
Shrimp Salad 25
Black Bean Salad 26
Salmon and Mixed Greens Salad with Walnuts 27
Chicken Salad with Carrots and Pistachios 28
Southwestern Grilled Chicken Salad 30
Provencal Chicken and Vegetable Salad 32
Chicken and Cashew Stir-Fry Salad 34
Roasted Sweet Potato Salad 36
Perfectly Grilled Chicken Breasts with Garlic, Lemon & Herbs 37
Healthy Veggie Salad 38
Mediterranean Baby Spinach Salad 39
Braised Kidney Beans & Sweet Potato 40
Grilled Chicken Caesar Salad 41
Chicken fried rice 42
Grilled Whole Trout with Lemon- Tarragon Bean Salad 43
Summer Greens and Strawberries with Poppy Seed Dressing 45
Summer Mediterranean Chickpea Salad 46
Turkey Avocado Cobb Salad 47
Fresh Lemon Greek Salad 48
Luscious Lime Shrimp Salad 49

HIGH PROTEIN LOW CARB

Minted Honey-Lime Fruit Salad 50
Barry's Orange Zest Summer Salad 51
Toasted Almond Chicken Salad.. 52
Summer Greens with Strawberries and Feta 53
Fresh and Filling Luncheon Salad 54
Tropical Pork Salad... 55
Summer Antipasto 56
Grapefruit, Mango, and Avocado Salad with Sherry Dressing 58
Zesty Summer Salad 59
Farmers' Market Vegetable Salad 60
Pan-Seared Salmon Salad 61
Turkey Chili Recipe.. 63
Grilled Chicken with Lime Butter Recipe 64
Simple Summer Chicken Recipe 66
Szechuan Peppers and Ground Turkey Recipe 67
Conclusion 68

HIGH PROTEIN LOW CARB

INTRODUCTION:

THE HIGH PROTEIN LOW CARB DIET RECIPES TO HELP TONE YOU UP AND GIVE YOU YOUR SLIM AND SEXY BODY THROUGH EVERY SEASON.

Are you ready to achieve the Badass Body of your dreams?
Ask yourself the number of times you started out on a new diet with the greatest of intentions of getting healthier and losing weight only for everything to fall apart faster than you can say.

Christmas Abbott a cross Fit celebrity is a living proof that fitness is sexy, and a badass body is a birthright for every one including you. She went further to shows you how to attain the body of your dreams with a targeted eating strategy i.e. eating the right protein, fat, carb. and total-body workout plan that will whip gluts and hips and every problem area into a top shape and sexy you.

Additionally, based on Christmas Abbot work with hundreds of clients at her Cross Fit gyms and nationwide fitness boot camps, she also offers specific detailed plans for every weight loss goal or building luscious curves on a "skinny fat" body. The Badass body diet will equip you with essential tools and motivation you need to build a healthy, vital body with the tight, firm tosh you've always wanted!

However, your gluts are the vast and most powerful muscle group in your body, not to mention one of the most beautiful. Many times they go dormant, flat, and flabby due to poor choices of lifestyle.

This high protein low carb Diet cookbook is packed with information on the right proteins, fats, and carbs otherwise known as "booty foods" all recommended in the Badass body diet.
This book is a great sit-down read, as well as a beginner's guide to the Badass body diet recipes. This book contains other "hacks" as described in the Badass body diet regime, which will make you feel really transform. I personally assure you that you will feel your best eating the high protein low

carb recipes that Christmas Abbot recommends in his book. I have recommended this type of diet to my clients and many have testified that the feel calmer, happier and have lost weight, without feeling hungry or unsatisfied.

This Cookbook will equip you on the right protein recipes to eat for your body type and fitness goals. It will make you improve your posture and functional mobility and enhance your overall health.

HIGH PROTEIN LOW CARB

THE BADASS RECOMMENDED RECIPES TO GIVE YOU THAT TIGHT BOOTY, SEXY ABS AND SKINNY LEGS

Badass Curried Chicken Fried "Rice" with Thai Coconut-Almond Sauce

Ingredients
4 Tablespoons of coconut oil
2 tablespoons of curry powder
2 teaspoons of chili powder
Sea salt and black pepper
1 small onion (diced)
2 cups of diced cooked chicken
2 Whole head of cauliflower
2 tablespoons of minced ginger
1 tablespoon of turmeric powder
2 tablespoons of red pepper flakes
1 each red and green pepper (diced)
4 eggs
4 cups of broccoli slaw
Thai Sauce Ingredients
6 tablespoons of lite coconut milk
2 tablespoons of liquid amino
½ cup of almond butter
2 teaspoons of apple cider vinegar

Directions
1. First, you "Rice" the cauliflower by grating it with the widest hole in a cheese grater.
2. After which you make the Thai sauce by whisking all ingredients together in a small bowl; set aside.
3. After that, you heat coconut oil over high heat in a wok or large fry pan.
4. Then you add the onions, spices and peppers and sauté a few minutes until translucent.

HIGH PROTEIN LOW CARB

5. This is when you add in the eggs and let them fry, breaking them up as you would have scrambled eggs.
6. Furthermore, you add the broccoli slaw and stir fry about 3-4 minutes.
7. Then you add the cauliflower rice and stir fry another 4-5 minutes.
8. Finally you add the diced chicken and Thai sauce.
9. After which you stir fry until the whole dish is heated through.

Cave girl Eats' Badass Chili

Ingredients
4 large links spicy Italian sausage (removed from casing)
2 (8-ounce) of can tomato sauce
2 cups of diced butternut squash (as for me I had to half-baked it ahead of time)
2 each red and yellow bell pepper (diced)
4 tablespoons of pumpkin seed butter
10 cloves garlic (minced)
4 tablespoons of chili powder
2 tablespoons of red pepper flakes
Sea salt and black pepper to taste
2 lbs. of grass-fed beef
2 (28-ounce) of can crushed tomatoes
1 ½ cups of red wine
2 (16 ounces) of mushrooms, sliced
2 shallot (diced)
2 tablespoons of cayenne pepper
2 tablespoons of cinnamon
2 tablespoons of coconut oil
4 tablespoons of cumin
4 tablespoons of cocoa powder

Directions
1. First, you sauté the shallots, beef, peppers, and sausage in the coconut oil over medium-high heat until tender and meat loses some of its pink.
2. After which you drain off the fat.
3. After that, you place meat, shallots and peppers in slow cooker.
4. Then you add in all of the remaining ingredients and blend together.
5. At this point, you cook on low for about 6-7 hours, stirring occasionally.
6. Finally, you serve alone, or over real spaghetti, or better still as I did over spaghetti squash.

Kenzie's Steak Salad

Ingredients:
½ cup of red onion
2 (4 ounces) of lean steak (grilled)
8 cups of Organic Spring Mix
4 Tablespoons of crumbled blue cheese
2 tomatoes (diced)

For the Dressing:
4 Tablespoons of balsamic vinegar, whisked with 2 Tablespoons of extra virgin olive oil

Directions:
First, you mix it all, after which you toss and enjoy!

Breakfast for Dinner

Ingredients:
4 cups of chopped fresh spinach
2 cups of sliced mushrooms
Salt and pepper to taste
4 tablespoons of olive oil for cooking
4 eggs, 8 egg whites, whisked (or better still Egg Beaters equivalent)
2 cups of pre-diced green peppers and onions
6 tablespoons of grated parmesan cheese (or crumbled feta)

Directions:
1. First, you heat olive oil over medium-high flame/burner in a medium sauté pan.
2. After which you add peppers and onions first, Sautee a few minutes until soft.
3. After that you add mushrooms, Sautee a few more minutes.
4. At this point, you pour eggs over the top of the veggies, and begin to scramble.
5. Then after a minute or so, when they just begin to set, you add in spinach and continue to scramble.
6. Furthermore, you add salt and pepper to taste.
7. Finally, you when they're done, sprinkle cheese over the eggs.

Note:
1. Remember, it can be eaten solo, or with whole wheat toast/English muffin.
2. For extra protein, I recommend you add low-fat turkey sausage to the scramble!

HIGH PROTEIN LOW CARB

No-Delivery Pizza

Ingredients:
Tomato sauce, in the jar
1 ½ cups of skim-milk mozzarella (shredded or crumbled reduced-fat feta)
4 whole-wheat English muffins (or better still 6-inch whole wheat pitas)
2 cups of pre-diced veggies (tomatoes, onions, green peppers, etc.)
1 cup of turkey pepperoni

Directions:
1. First, you toast the "crust" in a 350-degree oven for about 5 minutes.
2. After which you top with veggies, sauce, pepperoni and cheese.
3. After that, you turn oven up to 400 degrees and heat until the cheese is bubbly, about 8 minutes.
4. Finally, you then sever.

Note:
It is great when served with a quick-toss pre-bagged salad mix

Chicken-Black Bean-Rice Bowl

Ingredients:
2 cups of canned black beans (drained and rinsed)
2 cups of pre-diced green peppers and onions
2 cups of diced or shredded chicken breast meat (from a precooked rotisserie)
2 cups of brown rice, fast-cooking/microwaveable (or probably couscous)
1 cup of salsa (your preferred variety and level of spice)

Directions:
1. First, you prepare the rice or couscous as directed by the package.
2. After which you heat the chicken, black beans and veggies in the microwave, about 1 minute.
3. Then you combine the rice/couscous and remaining ingredients (including salsa).
4. Finally you serve!

HIGH PROTEIN LOW CARB

Hamm Cheese-Stuffed Chicken

Ingredients:
8 oz. skinless chicken breast
½ cup of low-fat, low-sodium cottage cheese
4 tablespoons of fresh rosemary
2 cups of chopped broccoli
2 tablespoons of olive oil
2 4-oz sweet potato
Nonstick cooking spray
2 light Laughing Cow Swiss cheese wedge
2/3 cup of diced tomato
4 tablespoons of oat bran
2 cups of chopped cauliflower
4 cloves garlic fresh (chopped)

Directions:
1. Meanwhile, you heat oven to a temperature of 350.
2. After which you spray a large baking dish with nonstick cooking spray.
3. After that, you cut chicken breast on half and set on baking dish.
4. Then you mash together the cheese wedge with cottage cheese in a small mixing bowl.
5. At this point, you add tomatoes and rosemary and then mix well.
6. Furthermore, you stuff the cheese mixture into one side of the chicken and use the other half breast to top it.
7. This is when you dust the top with oat bran.
8. After that, you toss together broccoli and cauliflower with oil and garlic in a separate bowl.
9. At this point, you place on the baking dish beside the chicken and bake chicken and vegetables for about 25 to 30 minutes.
10. In the meantime, you wash and poke a few holes in the potato with a fork.
11. After which you microwave for about 8 minutes (turning after 4 minutes).
12. Finally, you place the chicken breast, vegetables and sweet potatoes.
13. Then you serve with a vegetable such as asparagus.

Gluten Free Sweet Potato Muffins

Ingredients
6 eggs (lightly beaten)
4 tablespoons of olive oil
2 cups of brown rice flour
2 tablespoons of baking powder
2 tablespoons of ground cinnamon
¼ teaspoon of ground nutmeg
2 mediums sweet potato, roasted (about 3 cups, packed)
2 cups of unsweetened almond milk
1 cups of pure maple syrup
½ cup of coconut flour
1 teaspoon of kosher salt
2 teaspoons of ground ginger
¼ teaspoon of ground cloves

Directions:
1. Meanwhile, you heat the oven to 400 degrees F and lightly oil a 12-hole muffin tray.
2. After which you poke several holes in the sweet potato with a fork and wrap it in foil.
3. After that, you bake it in the oven for 60 minutes or until very soft.
4. This is when you remove potato from the oven and allow it to cool.
5. Then when cool enough to handle, you scrape the potato flesh out of the skin and mash it in a large mixing bowl (you either discard the skin or eat it).
6. Furthermore, you add the eggs, olive oil, almond milk, and maple syrup to the mixing bowl with the mashed potato and whisk everything together until smooth.
7. After which you combine the rest of the (dry) ingredients and stir together in a separate bowl.
8. At this point, you pour the dry ingredients into the bowl with the wet and mix together just until combined.

HIGH PROTEIN LOW CARB

9. In addition, you pour muffin batter into muffin holes and fill ¾ of the way up.
10. Finally, you place on center rack in the oven and bake for approximately 30 to 35 minutes or until muffins test clean.

Badass Blueberry Protein Pancakes

Ingredients:

2/3 cups of milk
2 scoop ON Cake Batter Whey
1 cup of blueberries
1 cup bisques mix
2 whole egg
2 tablespoons of vanilla extract

Directions:

1. First, you heat skillet to med-high heat and spray with non-stick spray
2. After which you mix all ingredients in bowl except for blueberries.
3. After that, you make sure to just stir the big chunks out, but do not stir too much.
4. Then you pour half of mixture into skillet and layer blueberries on top. Finally, you let it cook for about 1.5-2 minutes on each side.

Roasted Sweet Potato Soup

Ingredients

2 tablespoons of olive oil
6 cloves garlic
2-quart vegetable broth
3 teaspoons of yellow curry powder
1 teaspoon of ground sage
Salt to taste
2 large sweet potatoes, roasted (approximately 5 cups when pureed)
2 yellow onion (chopped)
3 cups of canned coconut milk (probably full fat)
2 tablespoons of fresh ginger (finely grated)
1 teaspoon of ground turmeric
¼ teaspoon of red pepper

Ingredients for the serving:
Chopped fresh cilantro
Drizzle of oil
Cooked quinoa
Plain yogurt/sour cream

Directions:
1. Meanwhile, you heat the oven to a temperature of 400 degrees F.
2. After which you poke holes in the sweet potato, wrap it in foil, and roast it in the oven for 60 minutes or until very soft.
3. After that, when sweet potato has finished roasting, allow it to cool then carefully scoop the flesh out the skin and place it in a blender (feel free to also leave the skin on).
4. At this point, you heat olive oil to medium in a medium skillet, and sauté the onion until translucent, about 10 minutes.
5. Then you add the garlic, curry powder, ginger, turmeric, red pepper, and sage, and sauté for another 2 minutes.
6. Furthermore, you add this mixture to the blender with the sweet potato, along with the chicken stock and coconut milk.

HIGH PROTEIN LOW CARB

7. After which you blend until smooth.
8. Then you add the soup back into the sauté pan (or better still large pot) to heat it to desired temperature.
9. Finally, you serve with cooked quinoa, fresh chopped cilantro, and plain yogurt (or probably sour cream).

Notes
Feel free to also use chicken broth

Twisted Tuna Salad

Ingredients
½ cup of carrot, finely chopped
½ cup of parsley, finely chopped
4 finely chopped scallions
½ cup plus 2 Tablespoons of mayonnaise
10 to 12 turns of black pepper, freshly ground
4 (5-ounce) cans of solid white albacore tuna (in water), drained very well
½ cup celery, finely chopped
⅓ Cup of red onion, finely chopped
1 small clove garlic (crushed)
1 teaspoon of kosher salt

Directions:
1. First, you drain the canned tuna very well.
2. After which you dump in to a large mixing bowl and set aside.
3. After that, you use the food processor with the chopping blade to process the following ingredients individually (carrot, celery, parsley, red onion and scallion.
4. Make sure you measure after chopping so you get the exact amount of each ingredient.
5. Then you add to bowl with tuna along with small clove garlic (crushed), mayonnaise, salt and pepper.
6. At this point, you use a fork to gently mash any very large chunks of tuna and then mix all the ingredients together.
7. Finally, you serve cold.

Chicken Caesar (The power salad)

Ingredients:
3 Tablespoons of grated Parmesan cheese
½ teaspoon of anchovy paste
½ teaspoon of Worcestershire sauce
6 cups of torn romaine lettuce
24 croutons (fat-free)
¼ cup of canola oil mayonnaise
2 Tablespoons of lemon juice
½-clove garlic (minced)
⅛ Teaspoon of black pepper
2 cups of cubed cooked boneless skinless chicken breast

Directions:
1. First, you combine the mayonnaise, Parmesan, lemon juice; anchovy paste, garlic, Worcestershire sauce, and pepper in a bowl and then mix well.
2. After which you combine the lettuce, chicken, and croutons in a separate bowl.
3. After that, you pour in the mayonnaise mixture and toss well to coat.
4. Then you divide among 4 bowls and serve.

Greek Salad

Ingredients:
One green pepper (sliced)
One cucumber (sliced)
Feta cheese (crumbled)
Grilled chicken or preferably fish (it is optional)
One head romaine lettuce (or you substitute your favorite lettuce)
2 ripe tomatoes (sliced)
Thinly sliced red onion (as many as you want)
Kalamata olives (as many as you want)
One handful toasted pine nuts

INGREDIENT FOR THE DRESSING
One tablespoon of fresh lemon juice
Pinch of oregano
4 Tablespoons of olive oil
One tablespoon of red wine vinegar
One slice fresh garlic (chopped or minced)
Salt and pepper to taste

Directions:
1. First, you clean, slice, and combine salad ingredients.
2. After which you mix dressing ingredients in a bowl, stirring with a fork, and give it the sniff test (if it smells too much of vinegar, I suggest you add more oil).
3. After that, you add to salad ingredients.
4. Then you toss and serve.
5. Enjoy!

Flank Steak Chopped Steakhouse Salad

Tips:
This recipe is an excellent source of protein and snooze-stopping iron.

Ingredients:
3/8 Teaspoon of salt
2 romaine lettuce hearts (chopped, about 6 cups)
1 cucumber (peeled, seeded, and chopped)
½ medium red onions (finely chopped)
¼ cup of crumbled blue cheese
½ teaspoon of Worcestershire sauce
1 lb. lean flank steak (trimmed)
3/8 Teaspoons of black pepper
4 plum tomatoes (seeded and chopped)
1 lg carrot (chopped)
⅓ Cup of reduced-fat crumbled blue cheese
1 Tablespoon of white wine vinegar
3 Tablespoons of light sour cream

Directions:
1. First, you prepare the grill for medium-high heat.
2. After which you sprinkle the flank steak with ¼-teaspoon salt and ¼-teaspoon pepper.
3. After that, you place the steak on a grill rack coated with cooking spray.
4. At this point, you grill 5 to 6 minutes per side, or until desired doneness and then transfer to a cutting board.
5. This is when you let rest for about 10 minutes before you slice thinly.
6. In the meantime, you combine the romaine, tomatoes, cucumber, carrot, and onion in a large bowl.

HIGH PROTEIN LOW CARB

7. After that, you combine the blue cheese, mayonnaise, sour cream, vinegar, Worcestershire sauce, and the remaining ¼-teaspoon of pepper in a separate bowl.
8. Then you add the cheese mixture to the romaine mixture and toss well to coat.
9. Finally, you divide among 4 serving bowls and top each with ¼ of the sliced steak.

Shrimp Salad

Tips:
1. Just a small serving of avocado in this recipe contains filling monounsaturated fat, which has a belly-flattening bonus.
2. A combination of that with a low-cal, protein-packed shrimp, and you have a satisfying lunch or dinner.

Ingredients:
½ teaspoon of salt
3 Tablespoons of extra virgin olive oil
2 grapefruit (cut into segments)
10 oz. of precooked shrimp
4 teaspoons of chopped cilantro
2¼ Tablespoons of white wine vinegar
½ teaspoon of chili powder
3 cups of butter head lettuce (torn into pieces)
2 avocados (peeled and sliced)
1 scallion (including top, thinly sliced)

Directions:
1. First, you combine the vinegar, salt, and chili powder in small bowl and then whisk in oil.
2. After which you put lettuce on serving plate or 4 individual salad plates.
3. After that, you arrange grapefruit, avocado, and shrimp over lettuce.
4. Then you sprinkle with scallion and cilantro.
5. Finally, you drizzle salads with chili dressing.

HIGH PROTEIN LOW CARB

Black Bean Salad

Tips:
One cup of this recipe contains half you daily dose of hunger-crushing fiber and about 15 grams of protein.

Ingredients:
2 cans, about16 oz. each of black beans (rinsed and drained)
2 Tablespoons of minced red onions
2 Tablespoons of olive oil
1 teaspoon of minced garlic
Salt
Lettuce leaves
1 cup of whole-kernel corn
¼ cup of chopped fresh parsley
¼ cup of balsamic vinegar
1 teaspoon of lemon juice
1 teaspoon of honey (or preferably brown sugar)
Ground black pepper

Directions:
1. First, you combine the corn, beans, parsley, onions, vinegar, oil, lemon juice, garlic, and honey or brown sugar in a large bowl.
2. After which you let the salad marinate for about 30 minutes at room temperature.
3. Then you add salt and pepper to taste.
4. Finally, you arrange the lettuce leaves on 4 salad plates, and then spoon the salad over the lettuce.

Salmon and Mixed Greens Salad with Walnuts

Tips:
The salmon and walnuts in this recipe contain plenty of belly-filling omega-3s.

Ingredients:
¼ cup of chopped walnuts
1 teaspoon of walnut oil
¼ teaspoon of sea salt
Ken's Lite Accents Honey Mustard salad spray
8 cups of mixed baby greens, baby lettuces, or preferably mixed Mediterranean greens
1 Tablespoon of olive oil
2 teaspoons of balsamic vinegar
¾ lb. of salmon fillet

Directions:
1. First, you wash and spin the greens until very dry.
2. After which you heat a large skillet over medium heat.
3. After that, you add the walnuts and toast for a minute.
4. Then you remove the walnuts from the skillet and set aside.
5. At this point, you heat ½ tablespoon of the olive oil in the skillet over medium heat.
6. In addition, you add half of the greens and cook gently for up to a minute.
7. After which you place the greens in a medium salad bowl.
8. This is when you repeat with the remaining olive oil and greens.
9. After that, you toss the warmed greens with the walnut oil, balsamic vinegar, and salt.
10. Then you place an oven rack approximately 8" from the broiler element.
11. In the meanwhile, you heat the broiler on high and then place the salmon skin side down in an ovenproof dish.
12. Then coat the fish's surface with 8 sprays salad spray.
13. Broil for about 8 to 10 minutes, until the fish is just cooked, depending on thickness.
14. Finally, you cut the fish into 4 servings and place on top of the greens.

Chicken Salad with Carrots and Pistachios

Tips:
The unusual combination of grapes, carrots and pistachios add a fun sweet/savory flavor punch plus
Pistachios are rich in fiber, protein and heart-smart fat.

Ingredients:
1 Tablespoon of brown sugar
½ teaspoon of salt
2 (6 oz. each) boneless, skinless chicken-breast halves (cut crosswise in thin slices)
1 Tablespoon of cider vinegar
1 medium shallot (thinly sliced)
1 bunch of watercress (tough stems removed)
2 Tablespoons of unsalted shelled chopped pistachios
1 lb. lg carrots (peeled and cut into slices about 2 cups)
2 Tablespoons of extra-virgin olive oil
½ teaspoon of freshly ground black pepper
4 Tablespoons of snipped fresh chives (or preferably sliced scallion greens)
1 teaspoon of cider vinegar
2 cups of baby arugula
1½ cups of halved red seedless grapes

Note:
1. Meanwhile, you heat the oven to a temperature of 425°F.
2. After which you coat an 11" x 9" baking pan and a rimmed baking sheet with olive oil cooking spray.

Directions:
1. First, you place the carrots in the prepared baking pan.

HIGH PROTEIN LOW CARB

2. After which you sprinkle with the sugar, 1 teaspoon of the olive oil, and ⅛ teaspoon each of the salt and pepper.
3. After that, you toss to coat thoroughly.
4. At this point, you roast, stirring several times, for about 25 minutes, until the carrots are tender and lightly golden at the edges.
5. Then at about 5 minutes before the carrots are done, you then place the chicken in a mound on the prepared baking sheet.
6. In addition, you drizzle with 1 teaspoon of the oil, and sprinkle with 2 tablespoons of the chives, and ⅛ teaspoon each of the salt and pepper.
7. You toss to mix and then arrange in a single layer.
8. After which you roast, turning once, for about 5 to 7 minutes, until cooked through.
9. Then you remove carrots, chicken from the oven, and let cool a few minutes.
10. In the meantime, you mix the vinegar, shallot, and the remaining oil, 2 tablespoons chives, and ¼ teaspoon each salt and pepper in a salad bowl.
11. After that, you let stand for about 5 minutes or more to blend the flavors.

Directions on how to finish the salad

1. First, you add the arugula, watercress, and grapes to the dressing and toss to mix well.
2. After which you spread out on a platter.
3. Then you top with the carrots, the chicken and any juices, and sprinkle with the pistachios.
4. Make sure you serve warm.

Southwestern Grilled Chicken Salad

TIPS:
1. This recipe is going to get you full on protein, fiber, and flavor with this Tex-Mex Salad.
2. The combination of corn, black beans, and lettuce provides more than one-third of your daily dose of fiber.

Ingredients for the Dressing
2 Tablespoons of chopped fresh cilantro
¼ cup of mild green salsa
¼ cup of light ranch dressing
Ingredients for the Salad
1 Tablespoon of chili powder
¼ teaspoon of ground cumin
¼ teaspoon of garlic powder
¼ teaspoon of onion powder
¼ teaspoon of salt
⅛ Teaspoon of ground black pepper
1 lb. of thin chicken breast slices (or preferably chicken tenders)
1 lime (quartered)
6 cups of shredded romaine lettuce
1 can (15 oz.) of black beans (rinsed and drained)
½ cup of corn kernels
1 medium tomato (chopped)
¼ cup of thinly sliced red onion

DIRECTIONS ON HOW TO MAKE THE DRESSING:
1. First, you mix the ranch dressing, salsa, and cilantro in a small bowl until blended.
2. After which you cover and refrigerate.

DIRECTIONS ON HOW TO MAKE THE SALAD:

HIGH PROTEIN LOW CARB

1. First, you coat a barbecue grill or ridged grill pan with olive oil spray, and heat to medium-hot.
2. After which you mix the chili powder, cumin, garlic powder, onion powder, salt, and pepper in a cup.
3. After that, you rub evenly on both sides of the chicken.
4. At this point, you grill the chicken, turning once, for about 3 to 4 minutes, or until it is no longer pink and the juices run clear.
5. Then you transfer to a plate and then squeeze the lime over the cooked chicken.
6. This is when you toss the romaine with half the dressing in a large bowl.
7. In addition, you divide among 4 plates.
8. After which you sprinkle the beans, corn, tomato, and red onion equally over each serving and top with the grilled chicken.
9. Finally, you serve the remaining dressing on the side.

Provencal Chicken and Vegetable Salad

Note that people who eat protein-rich eggs for breakfast were more satisfied and less like to nosh throughout the day compared to those who ate a bagel for breakfast.

Ingredients:
Breaded Dijon Chicken Breasts
Olive oil
2 teaspoons of herbs de Province
½ cup of Dijon mustard
3 cups of dried breadcrumbs
2 teaspoons of paprika
4½ lbs. of boneless, skinless chicken breast halves
Provencal Chicken-And-Vegetable Main Dish Salad
1 bag (about 5 oz.) of spring salad mix
½ cup of drained pre-sliced roasted red bell peppers
¾ cup of French vinaigrette salad dressing
½ bag (about 8 oz.) of prêt rimmed green beans (2 c)
4 Breaded Dijon Chicken Breasts (thinly sliced)
3 pre-hard-cooked eggs (sliced)
1 bunch of scallions (white and light green parts, sliced about ⅓ c)

DIRECTIONS ON HOW TO MAKE CHICKEN:
Combine the Breaded Dijon Chicken Breasts, olive oil, 3 cups of dried breadcrumbs, 2 teaspoons of herbs de Province, 2 teaspoons of paprika and 4½ lb. boneless, skinless chicken breast as follows:
1. First, you arrange two shelves in the center of the oven.
2. Meanwhile, you heat the oven to a temperature of 400°F.
3. After which you drizzle oil generously onto two 17" x 11" baking pans or other large shallow baking pans.
4. After that, you combine the breadcrumbs, herbs, and paprika on a large sheet of waxed paper.

HIGH PROTEIN LOW CARB

5. In addition, you lay the chicken in a single layer on another large sheet of waxed paper.
6. At this point, you coat both sides evenly with the mustard.
7. Then one at a time, you dip both sides of the chicken into the breadcrumb mixture.
8. Furthermore, you shake off any excess.
9. After which you place in a single layer on the prepared pans and then drizzle with oil.
10. After that, you bake for about 15 minutes.
11. Rotate the pans and then bake for 10 minutes longer, or until a thermometer inserted into the thickest portion registers 160°F and the juices run clear.
12. At this point, you set aside 4 chicken breast halves to use in the Provencal Chicken-And- Vegetable Main Dish Salad recipe below.

13. Remember to reserve the remaining Breaded Dijon Chicken Breasts and you let stand to cool completely.
14. Then you place in a zipper-lock bag and then refrigerate for up to 3 days for use later.

DIRECTIONS ON HOW TO MAKE THE SALAD:
1. First, you place the beans in an 8" x 8" microwaveable baking dish.
2. After which you add enough water to come ¼" up the sides of the dish.
3. After that, you cover with plastic wrap, leaving a small corner vent.
4. Then you microwave on high power for about 6 minutes, or until the beans are crisp-cooked.
5. At this point, you drain and rinse with cold water to stop the cooking.
6. This is when you pat dry and let stand to cool.
7. In the meantime, you arrange the spring mix on a large serving platter.
8. Finally, you top with the chicken, peppers, eggs, scallions, and the reserved beans.
9. Then you drizzle the dressing over the salad.

Chicken and Cashew Stir-Fry Salad

This recipe is full of good-for-you, monounsaturated fats and with a serving of skinless chicken breast, which gives it a hearty and flavor-packed.

Ingredients:
4 Tablespoons of reduced-sodium soy sauce
3 Tablespoons of raw cashews
5 cloves garlic (slivered)
1 lg red bell pepper (cut into thin strips)
4 scallions (diagonally sliced)
3 cups of baby spinach
12 oz. boneless, skinless chicken breast halves (cut into thin crosswise strips)
½ teaspoon of crushed red-pepper flakes
2 Tablespoons of olive (or preferably canola oil)
1½ Tablespoons of slivered peeled fresh ginger
2 medium carrots (cut into thin slices)
½ cup of orange juice
3 cups of shredded iceberg lettuce

Directions:
1. First, you mix the chicken, 2 tablespoons of the soy sauce, and the red-pepper flakes in a medium bowl, cover and set aside.
2. after which you cook the cashews in a small nonstick skillet over medium heat, stirring often, for about 3 to 4 minutes, or until lightly toasted.
3. After that, you tip onto a plate and let cool.
4. Then you heat 1 tablespoon of the oil in a large nonstick skillet over medium-high heat.
5. In addition, you add the garlic and ginger and stir-fry for about 1 to 2 minutes, or until fragrant and lightly golden.
6. After that, you add the chicken and stir-fry for about 3 to 4 minutes, or until no longer pink.
7. This is when you transfer to a clean bowl.
8. At this point, you place the remaining 1-tablespoon oil in the same skillet and heat over medium-high heat.

HIGH PROTEIN LOW CARB

9. After which you add the bell pepper and carrots, and stir-fry for about 3 minutes.
10. Furthermore, you add the scallions and stir-fry for about 2 minutes longer or until the vegetables are crisp-tender.
11. Then you return the chicken and any juices to the skillet.
12. After which you add the orange juice and the remaining 2 tablespoons soy sauce.
13. After that, you bring to a boil, stirring and then let boil for about 30 seconds.
14. Then you remove from the heat.
15. Finally, you mix the lettuce and spinach on a large, deep platter or in a wide, shallow bowl.
16. Then spoon the chicken mixture on top and sprinkle with the cashews.
17. Make sure you serve immediately.

Roasted Sweet Potato Salad

Ingredients:
¼ teaspoons of salt
2 lb. of sweet potatoes (scrubbed and cut into 1" chunks)
1 lb. of spinach or arugula (torn into bite-size pieces)
2 Tablespoons of olive oil
¼ teaspoon of freshly ground black pepper
2 lg of red bell peppers (cut into 1" pieces)
2 Tablespoons of white balsamic (or preferably white wine vinegar)

Directions:
1. Meanwhile, you heat the oven to a temperature of 425°F.
2. After which you combine the oil, salt, and black pepper in a large roasting pan.
3. After that, you add the sweet potatoes and bell peppers and toss to coat well.
4. Then you roast, stirring occasionally, for about 40 minutes, or until the potatoes are tender.
5. At this point, you remove from the oven and stir in the vinegar.
6. In addition, you place the spinach or arugula in a large serving bowl.
7. Then you add the potato mixture and toss to coat well.
8. Make sure you serve immediately.

Perfectly Grilled Chicken Breasts with Garlic, Lemon & Herbs

Ingredients
12 tablespoons of extra virgin olive oil
2 teaspoons of dried thyme
2-1/2 teaspoons of salt
3 teaspoons of lemon zest (from one lemon)

Directions:
1. First, you place chicken breasts between 2 pieces of wax paper and, using a meat mallet, pound to an even ½-inch thickness.
2. After which you mix the entire ingredients except chicken together in a 1-gallon zip-lock bag.
3. After that, you add chicken breasts and massage marinade into meat until evenly coated.
4. At this point, you seal the bag and place in a bowl in the refrigerator (the bowl will protect it against leakage).
5. Then you let the chicken marinate at least 4 hours or up to 12 hours.
6. In addition, you clean grill and preheat to high.
7. After which you lightly dip a wad of paper towels in vegetable oil and, using tongs, carefully rub over grates several times until glossy and coated.
8. Then you place chicken breasts on the grill (make sure they are well coated with the marinade).
9. Finally, you grill, covered, for about 2-3 minutes per side.

Healthy Veggie Salad

Tips:
This recipe can carry you through the entire afternoon.

Ingredients:
4 oz. low-fat cheddar cheese
1cup of tomato (diced)
½ cup of avocado (diced)
6 Tablespoons of sunflower seeds
8 cups of mixed salad greens
1 cup of cucumber slices
1 cup of sliced red bell pepper
2 cups of garbanzo beans
1 cup of crimini mushrooms
Ingredient for the dressing
2 teaspoons of lemon juice
Salt and pepper to taste
2 tablespoons of extra virgin olive oil

Directions:
1. First, you combine the entire ingredients.
2. After which you toss with olive oil and lemon juice.
3. Then you add salt and pepper to taste.

Mediterranean Baby Spinach Salad

Feel free to add other ingredients you have on hand to suit your personal taste.

Ingredients:
2 hardboiled eggs, preferably organic (sliced in half lengthwise)
1 cup of feta cheese (crumbled)
2 cups of garbanzo beans
6 tablespoons of extra virgin olive oil
Sea salt and pepper to taste
16 cups fresh baby spinach
12 olives
2 cups of whole cherry tomatoes (chopped)
4 tablespoons of red bell pepper (sliced)
2 tablespoons of fresh lemon juice
Optional: onions, anchovies, avocado, crimini mushrooms

Directions:
First, you divide spinach onto two plates and top each serving with half of the remaining ingredients.

Braised Kidney Beans & Sweet Potato

Ingredients:
8 medium cloves garlic (chopped)
2 medium carrots (sliced thin)
4 cups sweet potatoes (cut in 1-inch cubes)
1 teaspoon of cinnamon
2 teaspoons of paprika
2 tablespoons + 4 cups of vegetable broth
Salt & black pepper to taste
2 medium onions (chopped)
2 tablespoons of fresh ginger (chopped)
2 mediums green bell pepper (cut in 1-inch squares)
4 cups crimini mushrooms (sliced medium thick)
2 teaspoons of red chili powder
2 tablespoons of tomato paste
4 cups of cooked or preferably 2 (15 oz.) can (no BPA) kidney beans, drained

Directions:
1. First, you chop garlic, onions, and let sit for at least 5 minutes to bring out their hidden health benefits.
2. After which you heat 2 tablespoons of broth in a medium-large soup or braising pot.
3. After that, you healthy Sauté onion in broth over medium heat for about 4-5 minutes, stirring frequently, until translucent.
4. Then you add garlic, ginger, carrot, pepper, sweet potatoes, and mushrooms and continue to sauté for another 5 minutes, stirring frequently.
5. In addition, you add spices and mix thoroughly.
6. At this point, you mix tomato paste and broth together, then cover, and simmer on low for about 30 minutes stirring occasionally.
7. Finally, you add beans, salt, pepper, and continue to cook for another 5 minutes on medium heat uncovered, or until vegetables are tender.

Grilled Chicken Caesar Salad

Tips:
This recipe is far lighter, and just as good, as the popular full- fat version.

Ingredients
2 teaspoons of canola oil
Freshly ground pepper, to taste
2 cups of fat-free croutons
Lemon wedges
2 pounds boneless, skinless chicken breasts, trimmed of fat
½ teaspoon of salt (or to taste)
16 cups washed, dried and torn romaine lettuce
1 cup Caesar Salad Dressing
1-cup Parmesan curls

Directions:
1. First, you prepare a grill or preheat broiler.
2. After which you rub chicken with oil and season with salt and pepper.
3. After that, you grill or broil chicken until browned and no trace of pink remains in the center, for about 3 to 4 minutes per side.
4. At this point, you combine lettuce and croutons in a large bowl, then toss with Caesar Salad Dressing, and divide among plates.
5. Then you cut chicken into 1/2-inch slices and fan over salad.
6. Finally, you top with Parmesan curls and then serve immediately, with lemon wedges.

Note:
1. To make parmesan curls, I suggest you start with a piece of cheese that is at least 4 ounces.
2. Make sure you use a swivel-bladed vegetable peeler to shave off curls.

Chicken fried rice

Ingredients:
4 tablespoons of sweet chili sauce
4 tablespoons of peanut oil
2 brown onion (cut into thin wedges)
4 eggs (lightly beaten)
2 cups of Thai basil leaves
½ cup of fried shallots
4 tablespoons of light soy sauce
4 tablespoons of oyster sauce
2 (600g) chicken breast fillets, trimmed, thinly sliced
4 garlic cloves (crushed)
6 cups of cold cooked Sun Rice White Medium Grain Rice
8 green onions (sliced diagonally)

Directions:
1. First, you combine soy sauce, sweet chili sauce and oyster sauce in a small bowl and set aside.
2. After which you heat a wok over high heat until hot.
3. After that, you add 6 teaspoons oil and swirl to coat.
4. Then you add half the chicken and stir-fry for about 2 minutes or until browned.
5. At this point, you transfer to a plate and repeat with oil and remaining chicken.
6. In addition, you add remaining 4 teaspoons oil and onion to wok.
7. After which you stir-fry for about 2 to 3 minutes or until golden.
8. Then you add garlic and stir-fry for about 30 seconds.
9. This is when you add eggs and rice then stir-fry for about 2 to 3 minutes or until egg is well combined with rice.
10. Furthermore, you return chicken to wok and then add soy sauce mixture, basil and green onions.
11. Finally, you stir-fry for about 1 to 2 minutes or until well combined.
12. Then you spoon into bowls and sprinkle with fried shallots before you serve.

Grilled Whole Trout with Lemon-Tarragon Bean Salad

Note:
When you grill with the skin on it keeps the fish from falling apart and gives the skin a delightful crispy texture.

Ingredients
6 tablespoons lemon juice
2 tablespoons of chopped shallot
½ teaspoon of sugar
2 (15-ounce) can small white beans, rinsed
24 thin slices of lemon, (1-2 lemons)
½ cup of chopped fresh tarragon (plus 8 whole sprigs)
4 tablespoons of extra-virgin olive oil
2 teaspoons of kosher salt, divided
½ teaspoon of freshly ground pepper, divided
2/3 cup of chopped roasted red peppers
8 cleaned whole rainbow trout, (about 5 ounces each)

Directions:
1. First, you whisk chopped tarragon, lemon juice, oil, shallot, ½-teaspoon salt, sugar and ¼-teaspoon pepper in a medium bowl until combined.
2. After which you reserve 4 tablespoons of the dressing, then add beans and peppers to the rest.
3. After that, you toss to combine.
4. Meanwhile, you heat grill to medium-high and coat a large fish-grilling basket with cooking spray.
5. At this point, you stuff each trout with 6 slices lemon and 2 tarragon sprigs.
6. After which you sprinkle inside and out with the remaining 11/4 teaspoons salt and ¼ teaspoon pepper.
7. Then you place in the basket.
8. In addition, you grill the fish until the skin is golden and crispy, for about 4 to 5 minutes per side.

HIGH PROTEIN LOW CARB

9. After that, you carefully remove the lemon and tarragon, drizzle the fish with the reserved dressing.
10. Make sure you serve with the bean salad.

Summer Greens and Strawberries with Poppy Seed Dressing

Ingredients:
3 cups of torn arugula leaves
¼ cup of orange juice
½ teaspoon of grated orange rind
3 cups of watercress leaves
3 cups of sliced strawberries
2 teaspoons of olive oil
2 teaspoons of poppy seeds

Directions:
1. First, you combine the watercress, arugula, and strawberries in a large bowl.
2. After which you whisk the orange juice, oil, poppy seeds, and orange rind together in a small bowl.
3. Finally, you pour the dressing over the salad and toss gently to combine.

HIGH PROTEIN LOW CARB

Summer Mediterranean Chickpea Salad

Ingredients:
½ small red onion (quartered and thinly sliced)
A roasted red pepper (chopped)
2 Tablespoons of chopped parsley
3 Tablespoons of lemon juice
¼ teaspoon of salt
1 can (15 oz.) of chickpeas (rinsed and drained)
½ cucumber (peeled, seeded, and chopped)
3 plum tomatoes (chopped)
2 teaspoons of extra-virgin olive oil
2 cloves garlic (chopped)

DIRECTIONS:
1. First, you combine the entire ingredients in a large bowl.
2. After which you toss to mix.
3. Then you allow standing at room temperature for about 10 minutes for flavors to blend.

Turkey Avocado Cobb Salad

Ingredients:
2 tablespoons of olive oil
4 tablespoons of cider vinegar
16 cups of baby spinach leaves
A ripe avocado (cut into ½" cubes)
2 oz. blue cheese (crumbled)
2 lbs. of turkey breast cutlets
½ teaspoon of salt
2 teaspoons of Dijon mustard
8 slices of cooked reduced sodium turkey bacon, crumbled
8 cherry tomatoes (halved)

DIRECTIONS:
1. First, you preheat grill pan on medium high heat for about 2 minutes.
2. After which you brush turkey with 2 teaspoons of the oil and sprinkle with half of the salt.
3. After that, you grill turkey for about 4 minutes, flip, and continue cooking until centers are opaque and juices run clear, about 3 minutes longer.
4. Then you cut into chunks.

DIRECTIONS ON HOW TO PREPARE THE DRESSING:
1. First, you combine vinegar, mustard, 2 tablespoons of water, and remaining 4 teaspoons oil and ¼-teaspoon salt in glass jar.
2. After which you shake thoroughly.
3. Then you toss the spinach with 4 tablespoons of the dressing in large bowl.
4. At this point, you arrange turkey, bacon, avocado, tomatoes, and cheese over spinach.
5. Finally, you drizzle remaining dressing over salad and season with black pepper to taste.

Fresh Lemon Greek Salad

Tips:
This nonfat yogurt-based dressing provides probiotics, healthy bacteria, which boost your immune system.

Ingredients:
2 cups of torn escarole or curly endive
½ cup of thinly sliced radishes
4 tablespoons of lemon juice
2 tablespoons of nonfat plain yogurt
½ teaspoon of dried oregano
Ground black pepper, to taste
6 cups of torn romaine lettuce
½ cup of thinly sliced red onions
2 medium tomatoes (cut into 8 wedges)
4 teaspoons of olive oil
2 teaspoons of honey
Salt

Directions:
1. First, you combine the lettuce, escarole or endive, onions, radishes, and tomatoes in a large salad bowl.
2. After which you combine the lemon juice, oil, yogurt, honey, and oregano in a jar; shake to combine.
3. Finally, you add salt and pepper to taste and then pour over the salad; toss thoroughly.

Luscious Lime Shrimp Salad

TIPS:
This omega-3-rich fish like shrimp keep you sharp, focused, and mentally agile.

Ingredients:
2 tablespoons of chopped cilantro
1 tablespoon of hoi sin sauce
½ teaspoon of minced garlic
16 oz. large shrimp (peeled, deveined, and rinsed)
Bibb lettuce leaves
3 tablespoons of lime juice (preferably freshly squeezed)
2 small scallions, white and green parts (chopped add to shopping list)
1 teaspoon of extra-virgin olive oil
Pinches of ground white pepper
2 tablespoons of chopped red bell pepper

DIRECTIONS:
1. First, you combine the lime juice, cilantro, scallion, hoisin sauce, oil, garlic, and white pepper in a large bowl.
2. After which you whisk to mix and then set aside.
3. After that, you warm 2 tablespoons of the reserved mixture in a large nonstick skillet over medium heat and then add the shrimp.
4. At this point, you cook, tossing, for about 2 to 3 minutes, or until the shrimp are opaque.
5. Then you pour the skillet contents into the reserved mixture.
6. This is when you add the bell pepper, cover and refrigerate, tossing occasionally, for about 30 minutes.
7. Finally, you line each chilled plate with the lettuce leaves.
8. After which you spoon the shrimp and some of the marinade onto the lettuce.

Minted Honey-Lime Fruit Salad

Tips:
This salad is refreshing, sweet, and nutritious enough for breakfast and tasty enough for an afternoon snack.

Ingredients:
2 Tablespoons of lime juice
3 Tablespoons of chopped fresh mint
½ cantaloupes (cubed)
2 cups of fresh pineapple (or preferably mango cubes)
1 teaspoon of grated lime peel
4 Tablespoons of honey
½ small honeydew (cubed)
1 pint of fresh strawberries (halved and hulled)

DIRECTIONS:
1. First, you stir the lime peel, juice, honey, and mint in a large bowl until combined.
2. After which you add the honeydew, cantaloupe, strawberries, and pineapple or mango.
3. Finally, you toss to combine.

HIGH PROTEIN LOW CARB

Barry's Orange Zest Summer Salad

Ingredients for the salad
3 cups of mixed fruit (such as grapes, sliced kiwi, sliced strawberries, and cubed)
1 cup of mandarin oranges (drained)
4 cups of mixed salad greens
Mango, cantaloupe, honeydew, or watermelon
Ingredient for the Dressing
1 teaspoon of orange zest
½ teaspoon of lemon juice
1 Tablespoon of sugar or honey
½ cup of orange juice
1 cup of plain yogurt
2 Tablespoons of mayonnaise

DIRECTIONS TO MAKE THE SALAD:
First, you toss the greens, fruit, and mandarin oranges in a large bowl.

DIRECTIONS TO MAKE THE DRESSING:
1. First, you combine the orange juice, orange zest, yogurt, lemon juice, mayonnaise, and sugar in a small bowl.
2. After which you whisk together just before serving.
3. Finally, you pour over the salad, toss gently, and serve immediately.

Toasted Almond Chicken Salad

Ingredients:
6 ribs of celery (sliced)
1 cup of low-fat plain yogurt
3 teaspoons of dried tarragon
Ground black pepper, to taste
2 bags (10 oz.) mixed greens
6 small chicken breast halves
2 bunches chives (finely chopped)
½ cup of light sour cream
4 tablespoons of slivered almonds, toasted
Salt

Directions:
1. First, you coat a nonstick skillet with cooking spray and place over medium-high heat.
2. When it is hot, you add the chicken and cook for about 4 minutes per side, or until the juices run clear.
3. After that, you remove the chicken from the heat and let it rest for at least 10 minutes.
4. At a point, when they are cool enough to handle, you chop the chicken breasts into small pieces.
5. After which you combine the chicken, celery, chives, yogurt, sour cream, and tarragon in a large bowl and then mix lightly.
6. Finally, you cover and refrigerate for at least 1 hour, or up to 24 hours.
7. Then you add the almonds, and salt and pepper to taste and serve on a bed of greens.

Summer Greens with Strawberries and Feta

Tips:
The combination of the Herb sprigs chives and mint mix with heart-disease fighting strawberries for a healthy and sweet-smelling meal.

Ingredients:
1 cup of herb sprigs (such as chives, chervil, and mint)
½ cup of sliced small strawberries
12 cups of assorted lettuce greens (rinsed and dried well in a salad spinner)
3 Tablespoons of sherry vinaigrette
1 cup of crumbled goat (or sheep's milk feta)

DIRECTIONS:
1. First, you place the greens and herbs in a large bowl.
2. After which you add vinaigrette and gently toss to coat.
3. After that, you taste and add additional vinaigrette, if you wish.
4. Finally, you top with feta and berries, and serve.

Fresh and Filling Luncheon Salad

Tips:
This is a rice cakes substitute for carb-rich croutons and crumbled blue cheese replaces cheddar in this healthier version of a traditional chef salad.

Ingredients:
4 tablespoons of lemon juice (or balsamic vinegar)
2 head romaine lettuce, torn
2 carrots (thinly sliced)
1 small cucumber (sliced)
2 tablespoons of crumbled blue cheese
4 brown rice cakes (crumbled)
½ cup of low-fat mayonnaise salad dressing
½ teaspoon of black pepper
2 cups of sliced cooked chicken or beef
2 tomatoes (coarsely chopped)
4 tablespoons of parmesan cheese (it is optional)
2 tablespoons of sunflower seeds (it is optional)

Directions:
1. First, you combine the salad dressing, lemon juice or vinegar, and pepper in a measuring cup.
2. After which you combine the lettuce, chicken or beef, carrot, tomato, cucumber, Parmesan (if using), blue cheese, and sunflower seeds (if using) in a large serving bowl.
3. Then you sprinkle with the rice cakes and drizzle with the dressing.
4. Finally, you toss to coat evenly.

HIGH PROTEIN LOW CARB

Tropical Pork Salad

Ingredients:
4 teaspoons of ground cumin
2 (12 oz.) pork tenderloin, cut into 1" strips
2 tablespoons of cold water
4 tablespoons of chopped fresh cilantro
2 tablespoons of honey
¼ teaspoon of crushed red-pepper flakes
1 ripe papaya (peeled, seeded, and cut into chunks)
8 cups (about 1 large bunch) of torn watercress or spinach
4 tablespoons of sliced natural almonds
2 cups of chicken broth
2 tablespoons of cornstarch
½ cup of apricot nectar
2 tablespoons of lime juice
½ teaspoon of freshly ground black pepper
4 cups of fresh pineapple chunks (or juice-packed canned pineapple, drained)
2 ripe mangos (peeled, seeded, and cut into chunks)

Directions:
1. First, you combine the salad dressing, lemon juice or vinegar, and pepper in a measuring cup.
2. After which you combine the lettuce, chicken or beef, carrot, tomato, cucumber, Parmesan (if using), blue cheese, and sunflower seeds (if using) in a large serving bowl.
3. Then you sprinkle with the rice cakes and drizzle with the dressing.
4. Finally, you toss to coat evenly.

Summer Antipasto

It is time to satisfy your Italian cravings with this almost no-cook, vegetable-heavy main dish.

Ingredients for the Dressing
4 tablespoons of olive oil
¼ teaspoon of dried basil
¼ teaspoon of ground black pepper
6 tablespoons of red wine vinegar (or balsamic vinegar)
1 clove garlic (minced)
¼ teaspoon of salt
Ingredient for the Salad
2 medium zucchini (cut into 2" matchsticks)
2 cups of cherry tomatoes, halved
2/3 cup of pitted Kalamata olives, pitted
32 slices turkey pepperoni
2 small bunch broccolis (cut into florets)
2 lbs. shrimp (cooked)
1 cup of canned artichoke hearts (drained and quartered)
2 (4 oz.) part-skim mozzarella cheese (cut into ½" cubes)
16 slices reduced-fat deli ham (rolled into tubes)

DIRECTIONS TO MAKE THE DRESSING:
First, you whisk the red wine or balsamic vinegar, oil, garlic, basil, salt, and black pepper in a small bowl.

DIRECTIONS TO MAKE THE SALAD:
1. First, you bring a medium saucepan of water to a boil.
2. After which you fill a large bowl with ice water and set near the stove.
3. After that, working in batches, you boil the broccoli and zucchini just until tender (they will turn bright green).
4. At this point, you use a slotted spoon to transfer the vegetables to the ice water to halt the cooking process and then drain well.
5. Then you place the shrimp in the center of a large platter.

HIGH PROTEIN LOW CARB

6. Finally, you arrange the broccoli, zucchini, tomatoes, artichoke hearts, olives, cheese, ham, and pepperoni in small mounds around the shrimp.
7. After which you drizzle with the dressing.

Grapefruit, Mango, and Avocado Salad with Sherry Dressing

Tips: This recipe is mixed with belly-flattening avocados with fiber-rich mangos and grapefruit for a tropical treat.

Ingredients:
2 tablespoons of medium-dry sherry (or preferably sherry vinegar)
½ teaspoon of salt
2 lg pink grapefruit
2 cups of sliced ripe avocado
4 tablespoons of chopped red onion
2 tablespoons of olive oil
3 teaspoons of red wine vinegar
¼ teaspoon of freshly ground black pepper
8 cups of colorful mixed baby greens
2 cups of sliced ripe mango

Directions:
1. First, you mix the oil, sherry or sherry vinegar, red wine vinegar, salt, and pepper in a salad bowl with a fork.
2. After which you use a serrated knife to peel the grapefruit, cutting off most, but not all, of the white pith.
3. After that, working over a bowl, you cut out the fruit from between the membranes.
4. Then you add 3 tablespoons of the grapefruit juice to the dressing and mix thoroughly.
5. Finally, you add the greens, avocado, mango, red onion, and the grapefruit sections to the dressing and toss gently to mix.
6. Make sure you serve immediately.

HIGH PROTEIN LOW CARB

Zesty Summer Salad

Tips:
Try marinating ingredients the night before a summer party and wow friends with this colorful and vitamin-A-rich passer.

Ingredients:
2 hothouse cucumbers (cut into 1" pieces)
½ cup of light Italian dressing
12 tablespoons of grated Parmesan cheese
6 lg tomatoes (cut into wedges)
8 scallions (thinly sliced)
Ground black pepper, to taste
12 lettuce leaves

DIRECTIONS:
1. First, you combine the tomatoes, cucumber, and scallions in a refrigerator container.
2. After which you add the dressing, and season to taste with salt and pepper; mix thoroughly.
3. Then you cover and refrigerate for about 4 hours or overnight, stirring the salad several times.

DIRECTIONS TO SERVE:
1. First, you drain off most of the dressing.
2. After which you place a lettuce leaf on each of the salad plates and spoon salad into each leaf.
3. Then you sprinkle 1 tablespoon Parmesan over each.

HIGH PROTEIN LOW CARB

Farmers' Market Vegetable Salad

Ingredients:
½ cup of vinegar
2 cups of whole cooked green beans
1 cup of sliced celery
1 medium Spanish onion (sliced)
½ cup of salad oil
½ cup of sugar
1 cup of sliced cooked carrots
1 cup of green pepper (sliced or cut into strips)

DIRECTIONS:
1. First, you prepare the dressing of oil, vinegar, and sugar mixed.
2. After which you mix green beans, carrots, celery, green pepper, and onion into dressing and keep pressed down with plate on top.
3. After that, you refrigerate overnight.
4. Finally, you drain well before serving.

Pan-Seared Salmon Salad

Tips:
This recipe is a mixture of balsamic vinegar, Dijon mustard and sundried tomatoes pair nicely with salmon for this omega-3-filled delight.

Ingredients:
6 tablespoons of balsamic vinegar
3 teaspoons of dried basil
¼ teaspoon of salt
2 lbs. mixed salad greens
2 small onions (minced)
2 teaspoons of Italian seasoning
6 tablespoons of chopped dry-pack sun-dried tomatoes
4 teaspoons of extra-virgin olive oil
2 teaspoons of Dijon mustard
2 roasted red pepper (cut into small strips)
2 (4 oz.) button or preferably shiitake mushrooms, sliced
8 salmon fillets (3 oz. each), skin removed

Directions:
1. First, you place the sun-dried tomatoes in a small bowl and then cover with boiling water.
2. Then you allow soaking for about 10 minutes, or until soft.
3. After which you drain and discard the liquid.
4. After that, you whisk the vinegar, oil, basil, mustard, and salt in a large bowl until smooth.
5. At this point, you place the pepper, sun-dried tomatoes, and greens in the bowl but do not toss and set aside.
6. Furthermore, you coat a medium nonstick skillet lightly with nonstick spray.
7. Then you add the mushrooms, onion, and then coat lightly with nonstick spray.
8. After which you cook over medium-high heat for about 5 to 7 minutes, or until soft.
9. After that, you remove to a plate to cool.

HIGH PROTEIN LOW CARB

10. This is when you wipe the skillet with a paper towel and then coat with nonstick spray.
11. After which you set over high heat and lightly coat the salmon with nonstick spray.
12. After that, you sprinkle with the Italian seasoning and add the salmon to the skillet.
13. Cook for about 3 minutes on each side, or until the fish flakes easily and check by cutting into 1 fillet.
14. Finally, you add the mushrooms and onion to the reserved bowl and toss to mix.
15. Then you spoon the salad onto 4 plates and top each with a salmon fillet.

HIGH PROTEIN LOW CARB

Turkey Chili Recipe

Ingredients
4 cups of carrots (sliced or diced)
4 bell pepper (chopped)
4 tablespoons of tomato paste
2 cups of chicken (or turkey stock)
2 tablespoons of ground cumin
2 teaspoons of dried oregano
Green onions, sliced (it is optional, for garnishing)
6 to 8 cups of shredded, cooked turkey meat
4 cups of onions (chopped)
4 cups of diced tomatoes
8 garlic cloves (minced)
4 tablespoons of chili powder or to taste
2 tablespoons of dried hot red pepper flakes
Paleo cooking fat
Sea salt and freshly ground black pepper to taste

Directions:
1. First, you melt some cooking fat in a large saucepan placed over a medium-high heat, and cook the onions, bell peppers and carrots for about 5 minutes until the onions are golden.

2. After which you add the garlic, chili powder, cumin, red pepper flakes, and oregano.

3. After that, you stir well and cook for a minute.

4. Then you add the tomato paste, diced tomatoes, chicken or turkey stock, cooked turkey meat, and season with salt and pepper to taste.

5. At this point, you give everything a good stir and then bring the chili to a simmer, reducing the heat to low, and let it simmer, uncovered, for about 30 to 45 minutes.

6. Make sure you serve warm with freshly sliced green onions on top.

Grilled Chicken with Lime Butter Recipe

Ingredients
2 tablespoons of chili powder
2 tablespoons of honey (it is optional)
6 tablespoons of olive oil
Sea salt and freshly ground black pepper to taste
7 to 8lb. bone-in chicken parts
2 tablespoons of ground cinnamon
2 teaspoons of unsweetened cocoa powder
2 tablespoons of balsamic vinegar
Ingredients for lime butter
1 cup of ghee (melted)
4 tablespoons of shallots (minced)
Freshly ground black pepper to taste
½ cup of chopped fresh cilantro
2 Serrano Chile, minced
2 tablespoons of fresh lime juice;

Directions:
1. Meanwhile, you heat your grill to a medium-high heat.

2. After which you combine the chili powder, ground cinnamon, cocoa powder, olive oil, balsamic vinegar, honey, if using, in a bowl and season with salt and pepper to taste.

3. After that, you mix until well blended.

4. At this point, you brush the chicken pieces with the sauce.

5. Then you place the chicken on grill and cook for about 30 min (or preferably, until the chicken is cooked; the exact time varies depending on what chicken parts you are using).

6. This is when you combine all the ingredients for the lime butter in a bowl.

HIGH PROTEIN LOW CARB

7. After which you drizzle the lime butter over the chicken before serving.

Simple Summer Chicken Recipe

Ingredients
1 cup of lemon juice
4 teaspoons of Italian seasoning
Sea salt and freshly ground black pepper to taste
8 skinless, boneless chicken breasts
1 teaspoon of onion powder
4 garlic cloves (minced)

Directions:
1. Meanwhile, you heat your grill to a medium-high heat.

2. After which you place the chicken in a marinating container (preferably, glass or ceramic; not metal) and drizzle with the lemon juice, onion powder, Italian seasoning, garlic.

3. After that, you season each breast to taste.

4. At this point, you let the chicken marinate for about 20 minutes.

5. Then you cook on the prepared grill for about 10 to 15 minutes per side, or until cooked through.

6. Make sure you serve warm with extra lemon wedges.

Szechuan Peppers and Ground Turkey Recipe

Ingredients
8 oz. of water chestnuts (sliced)
3 garlic cloves (minced)
½ cup of chicken stock
1 tablespoon of honey (it is optional)
1 tablespoon of rice wine vinegar
Cooking fat
1 lb. of ground turkey
1 lb. of bell peppers (sliced)
2 tablespoons of ginger (minced)
3 tablespoons of coconut amino
2 teaspoons of fish sauce
½ tablespoon of sriracha sauce (it is optional)

Directions:
1. First, you melt some cooking fat in a large wok placed over a medium-high heat.

2. After which you add the ground turkey, garlic, and ginger.

3. After that, you break down the turkey and cook until browned.

4. Then you combine the chicken stock, coconut amino, honey, fish sauce, rice wine vinegar and Sriracha sauce in a bowl.

5. At this point, you add the bell peppers and coconut amino mixture to the wok and cook for another 4 to 5 minutes.

6. Finally, you add the water chestnuts and cook for an additional 2 minutes, before you serve.

Conclusion

To lose weight is very easy if you know the process and how to go about it. That is the reason for this Book, to help you achieve your weight loss goal in No time. Get in shape while eating the foods you love. Take advantage of this recommended Badass body diet recipes provided for you in this book. Remember, the only bad action you can take is no action at all.

www.ingramcontent.com/pod-product-compliance
Lightning Source LLC
Chambersburg PA
CBHW080022130526
44591CB00036B/2581